SCIENCE FOR ROCKETING INTO SPACE

Mark Thompson

WAYLAND
www.waylandbooks.co.uk

Published in paperback in Great Britain in 2020
by Wayland
Copyright © Hodder and Stoughton, 2019
All rights reserved

Editor: Amy Pimperton
Design and illustration: Collaborate

ISBN: 978 1 5263 0811 5
Printed and bound in China

Wayland, an imprint of
Hachette Children's Group
Part of Hodder and Stoughton
Carmelite House
50 Victoria Embankment
London EC4Y 0DZ

An Hachette UK Company

www.hachette.co.uk
www.hachettechildrens.co.uk

The website addresses (URLs) included in this book were valid at the time of going to press. However, it is possible that contents or addresses may have changed since the publication of this book. No responsibility for any such changes can be accepted by either the author or the Publisher.

Note: In preparation of this book, all due care has been exercised with regard to the instructions, activities and techniques depicted. The publishers regret that they can accept no liability for any loss or injury sustained. Always get adult supervision and follow manufacturers' advice when using electric and battery-powered appliances.

CONTENTS

REACH FOR THE STARS

Do you think that you can jump high enough so that you can reach the Moon? Give it a try now, jump as high as you can and see if you can make it. If you are a great jumper then you might be able to jump as high as one metre, but you will probably not get much higher.

The force of gravity keeps us firmly stuck to Earth's surface, so if you want to get into space then you are going to need some help.

FAR-OUT IDEAS!

What do you think you could use? You could use a giant rubber band, a massive spring or maybe even shoot yourself out of a cannon. These ideas might get you a few more metres, but to get into space you are going to need something else – a rocket.

EARLY ROCKETS

The first rockets were made hundreds of years ago by the Chinese and Babylonians (the Babylonians were people of a region in what is now Iraq). They filled bamboo sticks with explosive powder and then threw them onto a fire to celebrate some exciting occasion. The bamboo sticks would give off a loud 'CRACK', and fly off in all directions. Very dangerous and definitely not something to try at home!

UP IN SMOKE

According to an ancient story, one brave Chinese emperor, called Wan Hu, decided to become the first space traveller by strapping 47 of these rockets to a chair!

He sat on the chair in his finest robes while the rockets were lit, there was a massive bang and clouds of smoke and he was never seen again! Maybe Wan Hu made it into space and never came back.

AWESOME ENGINEERING

Rockets today are far safer than Wan Hu's chair, and his chair would probably not help us get into space.

So that we can see how rockets send humans safely into space, we are going to look at how rockets work, how they lift off, how they can be made to fly in straight lines, their shape and what it would feel like to be inside a spacecraft floating around in weightlessness.

This book is full of fun experiments and investigations that explore how rockets work.

ESCAPE GRAVITY

To get into space, a rocket has to overcome the pull of Earth's gravity. It does this by travelling at around 11.2 km per second (km/s). Larger planets, such as Jupiter, usually have a stronger pull of gravity, which means a rocket is heavier there and must travel faster to overcome gravity. To explore gravity on Jupiter, we need to compare the weight of something on Earth with how much it would weigh on Jupiter.

YOU WILL NEED:

- two identical empty jam jars
- some sand
- a cup
- scales
- a notebook and pencil

SCIENCE FACT

Everything in the Universe is made of matter: a table, yourself, the Sun and Moon. The amount of matter in something is called its mass. The more mass something has, the stronger its gravitational pull. Anything made of matter pulls everything else made of matter towards it. Sometimes this pull is small so we don't notice it. Bigger gravitational pulls are more obvious, such as a ball being pulled to the ground by Earth's gravity.

1 Take one jam jar and put a cup of sand in it.

2 Place the jam jar on the scales. Make a note of its weight in kg.

3 Jupiter is the most massive of all the planets in the Solar System, so it has the strongest effect of gravity. To work out how much your first jam jar would weigh on Jupiter, multiply its weight by 2.34. Make a note of the answer.

4 Place the second empty jam jar on the scales. Fill it with sand until it weighs the same as your answer from step 3.

5 Hold the jam jars and feel how much heavier the second one is compared with the first one. That's how much heavier the first one would be on Jupiter.

To escape Jupiter's gravity, a rocket would need to travel at 59.5 km/s, because it weighs much more there than on Earth.

CALCULATE
To find out how much you would weigh on Jupiter, multiply your weight by 2.34.

SPACE FACT
Black holes are dead stars. They have an incredibly strong gravitational pull. If you were trying to launch a rocket from one you would need to travel faster than the speed of light, which is 300,000 km/s!

OVERCOME INERTIA ... WITH AN EGG

When a rocket sits on its launch pad it has something called inertia. A rocket shooting through space also has inertia. Inertia describes how something does not want to change what it is doing. In the case of a rocket on a launch pad its engines are off, so it doesn't want to move. If it is zooming through space it wants to continue zooming through space. Before we can launch a rocket into space we must overcome its inertia. You can explore inertia with an egg!

YOU WILL NEED:

- a plastic beaker
- some water
- a shallow tray
- a short cardboard tube
- a fresh egg

RED ALERT!
This could get messy, so do it outside.

1 Fill the plastic beaker about three-quarters full of water.

2 Place the shallow tray on top of the beaker. Place the cardboard tube on top of the tray so that it is directly above the beaker.

3 Carefully place the egg on top of the cardboard tube. Notice what the egg is doing! It's doing nothing sitting on top of the tube. It has inertia, which means it does not want to start moving.

4 Hold the beaker on the ground. Hit the tray firmly with your other hand from one side so that it slides off the top. DO NOT strike downwards or upwards. The tray should be knocked horizontally off the top of the beaker.

5 The lip of the tray will knock the tube out from under the egg. The egg, which has inertia, resists any movement and, for a tiny fraction of a second, does nothing. Gravity soon overcomes the egg's inertia, and the egg drops into the water.

SPACE FACT

We get high tides because of the pull of gravity from the Moon. One high tide lies on the side of Earth closest to the Moon. On the opposite side another high tide occurs. This high tide is partly due to inertia. As Earth spins at around 1,673 km per hour (km/h), the inertia of the water trying not to move causes the high tide.

EXPLORE EPIC EXOTHERMIC ERUPTIONS

For a rocket to get into space, it needs something to push it. The pushing force comes from the explosive energy created by a chemical reaction between liquid hydrogen and liquid oxygen. This type of chemical reaction is exothermic, which means it gives off lots and lots of energy. Hydrogen is very dangerous though, so to explore chemical reactions we are going to use hydrogen peroxide to create an eruption of foam.

YOU WILL NEED:

- a mixing bowl and spoon
- three tablespoons of water
- four teaspoons of bakers' yeast
- a clean, empty two-litre drinks bottle
- a tray (optional)
- safety goggles
- a measuring jug or cup
- hydrogen peroxide, 9% strength, (available from chemist shops)
- washing-up liquid
- food colouring (optional)
- a small funnel (optional)

1 In a bowl, mix three tablespoons of warm water with four level teaspoons of yeast until it is a thick liquid.

2 Place the drinks bottle on a large tray. If you don't have one, place it on the ground, outside.

3 Put on your safety goggles DO NOT put your face over the bottle as you perform this experiment.

4

Pour 150 ml (about half a cup) of hydrogen peroxide into the drinks bottle.

5

Add a good squirt of washing-up liquid. You could add some food colouring at this stage too if you want colourful foam.

6

Use a funnel (if you have one), to pour the yeast mixture into the drinks bottle ... and stand back!

SCIENCE FACT

Hydrogen peroxide contains hydrogen and oxygen. The yeast causes a chemical reaction that breaks apart the hydrogen peroxide to form oxygen and water. The washing-up liquid traps the oxygen, creating loads of little bubbles. Notice how the bottle feels warm to the touch; the chemical reaction created heat, too, in an exothermic reaction. The foam and liquid are all safe to wash down the sink.

7

Watch as foam starts to build up until it pops out of the top of the bottle.

BALLOON TO THE MOON

Watching a rocket roar off a laur pad is an amazing sight. A rock on a launch pad is pulled dow to Earth by gravity. As soon as the rocket fires its engines, they create an unbalanced pushing force that is stronger than the force of gravity, so the rocket shoots upware

We measure force in Newtons. The engines on the *Saturn V* rocket that sent Neil Armstrong (1930–2012) to the Moon produced 33,400,000 Newtons! Even if you don't have a *Saturn V*, you can still explore forces with a balloon rocket!

YOU WILL NEED:

- a straw
- scissors
- a long piece of string (at least 5 m long)
- a balloon
- sticky tape

1 Cut the straw into a straight piece about 6 cm long.

6 cm

2 Thread the string through the straw.

SCIENCE FACT

Newtons are named after the scientist, Sir Isaac Newton (1642–1727). His third law of motion says: 'for every action there is an equal and opposite reaction'. Think of two friends, each standing on their own skateboard. If one friend gently pushes the other, then the friend who was pushed (the action) will move away, but the friend doing the pushing will also move away (the equal and opposite reaction).

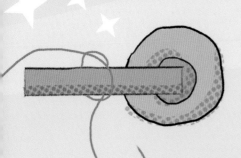

3

Tie one end of the string to a door handle or some other stable point that is easy to reach.

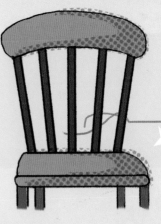

4

Pull the string tight and tie the other end to another point, such as a chair. Check that the straw slides along the string easily.

5

Blow up the balloon, but do not tie a knot in it. Instead, hold the end of the balloon tightly so that the air can't escape.

6

Ask a friend to stick the balloon to the straw with sticky tape while you are holding the air in the balloon.

7

Pull the balloon back to the end of the string so that the neck of the balloon is closest to one end of the string. Now the fun bit! Let go of the balloon and watch as Newton's third law of motion pushes the balloon along the string, just like a real rocket.

SPACE FACT

A *Saturn V* rocket weighs 2,800 tonnes, which is about the same as 400 elephants!

LOWER THE CENTRE OF GRAVITY

An object's centre of gravity is a point where all of its weight is concentrated and the object balances perfectly. An object can be made more stable and less likely to fall over by lowering its centre of gravity. A rocket on a launch pad is stable because its centre of gravity is concentrated above its base.

The position of a rocket's centre of gravity changes during flight as fuel gets used up and bits of the rocket fall away. Astronauts need to know where the rocket's centre of gravity is at all times to ensure the rocket is stable as it flies. In this fun experiment we play around with the centre of gravity of a pencil.

YOU WILL NEED:

- a pencil (sharpened)
- two pipe cleaners or pieces of garden wire about 15 cm long
- two clothes pegs

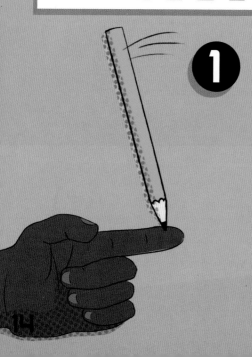

1 First, try to balance the pencil with its point on your finger. You won't be able to do it because the centre of gravity of the pencil is too high. At the moment it is about halfway up the length of the pencil.

2 Take a pipe cleaner, or a piece of garden wire, and wind one end around the pencil, about 1 cm above the point.

3 Repeat this with the other pipe cleaner or piece of wire, so that they are opposite each other and wound around the pencil at roughly the same point.

4 Clip a clothes peg on the end of each of the two pipe cleaners or pieces of wire.

5 Bend the pipe cleaners or wires so that they form an 'M' shape when you hold the pencil upright. The clothes pegs need to be lower than the point of the pencil.

6 Now try to balance the pencil point on your finger again. You should find that it now stays in place.

This works because we have moved the centre of gravity of the object to a point lower than your finger, which makes the object more stable.

Have a go at playing around with the position of the pegs and see if you can get the pencil to stand up on its end at an angle.

SPACE FACT

At launch, the *Saturn V* rocket stood about 100 m tall, but its centre of gravity was less than halfway up at just under 30 m from the ground.

BLAST OFF... WITH A CHEMICAL REACTION

Rockets are driven by powerful reactions between chemicals, such as liquid oxygen and liquid hydrogen (see pages 10–11). A chemical reaction is when one set of chemical substances is changed into another.

In this case, hydrogen and oxygen are changed into H_2O – water! The reaction creates loads of energy in the form of steam, which increases the pressure inside the rocket engine, pushing the rocket up into space. You can create the same effect with a film canister and an antacid tablet.

YOU WILL NEED:

- an antacid tablet – ask an adult for one (available from chemist shops)
- a film canister (these can be bought online or from photo processing shops on the high street – white ones work the best)
- some water
- a stopwatch or wristwatch with a second hand

1 Prepare for your launch by breaking an antacid tablet in half.

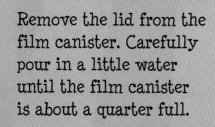

2 Remove the lid from the film canister. Carefully pour in a little water until the film canister is about a quarter full.

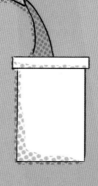

3 Take the film canister, lid and antacid tablet outside.

4 When you are ready to launch your rocket, place both halves of the antacid tablet into the canister, replace the lid, turn it upside down, put it on the ground and step back.

5 You will need to wait for up to about 30 seconds before the rocket will blast off.

6 When the water and antacid mix they produce carbon dioxide gas. The gas builds up inside the canister, causing the pressure to build up, too. The pressure gets so high that it forces the lid to pop off and the rocket to shoot up into the air.

SPACE FACT

There are many different types of rocket engine. Some use liquid fuel, some use solid fuel and others use more complicated engines that are powered by gas.

LAUNCH A STRAW ROCKET ... WITH PUFF POWER

Why are rockets rocket-shaped? Everything including air, is made up of tiny particles we cannot see, called molecules. Air molecules hit the rocket and slow it down as it tries to travel through them.

We call this effect drag, so rockets are shaped to cut through the air and hit as few air molecules as possible. This is done by designing rockets with a small surface area and an aerodynamic shape. In this activity, see how a rocket's design helps it to fly.

YOU WILL NEED:

- a sheet of A4 paper
- scissors
- a straw
- sticky tape
- a small sheet of coloured paper

1 Cut the sheet of A4 paper in half lengthways.

2 Roll one half lengthways around the straw, making sure it is not too tight. Fix it in place with sticky tape to make a tube.

3 Remove the straw and cut the paper tube so it is about 3 cm shorter than the straw. To make your rocket a more streamlined shape, neatly fold over the top, and secure it with tape.

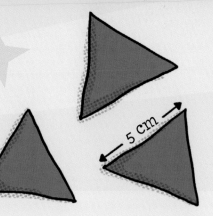

4 Cut out three triangles from the coloured paper. They should be about 5 cm along each side.

5 cm

5 To help your rocket balance, tape the triangles to the bottom of the paper tube, so that they are equally spaced around it.

6 Slip the tube over the straw, take a breath and blow hard. The tube rocket will blast off the end of the straw. Measure how far the rocket travels.

GO FURTHER

Experiment by attaching small pieces of modelling clay to the front or back to adjust your rocket's centre of gravity. See if this affects how far it can fly. You could record your measurements to find the best combination. How else could you improve your rocket's aerodynamic design?

SPACE FACT

Huge spacecraft travelling through space can have their direction adjusted by puffing small jets of gas out the side of the spacecraft. The force from the jets can be very small because there is no air resistance in space to act as drag.

HURTLE TO EARTH ON AN 'EGGCITING' MISSION

What goes up must also come down! Astronauts return to Earth in re-entry capsules that are shaped a little like an egg. Like rockets, these capsules are also designed to be aerodynamic and have a small surface area, so that they can travel quickly. They reach speeds of around 21,200 km/h!

But re-entry capsules have another important job. They have to slow down enough to land safely, otherwise the returning astronauts could be seriously hurt. This is where drag becomes useful. Let's look at the effect of drag on the surface area of your own capsule to see how you can make it land safely!

YOU WILL NEED:

- a bin bag
- scissors
- four 50-cm lengths of string
- a sandwich bag (with handles)
- two fresh eggs

1 Cut a square out of the bin bag about 50 cm by 50 cm. Tie a 50 cm piece of string tightly to each corner. This is your parachute.

2 Tie the other ends of the strings to the handles of the sandwich bag.

3 Place one of the eggs into the sandwich bag and check that it hangs securely below the parachute.

4 The next bit should be done – carefully – out of a bedroom window. Make sure no one is below first!

Drop the other egg out of the window. What happens to it? It will probably break when it hits the ground and make a big mess. It has a small surface area so travels through the air very fast.

5 Hold the parachute open with the egg dangling underneath. Now drop it. The parachute has a much larger surface area than the egg, so it experiences more drag, which slows the falling egg. It should land safely, just like a real capsule does when its parachute opens, moments before it hits the ground!

SPACE FACT

The International Space Station (ISS) was taken to space in bits and assembled there, so it never had to travel through Earth's atmosphere. This means it can be whatever shape it needs to be without worrying about drag. It isn't streamlined and instead looks like a crazy television aerial.

SEND A ROCKET INTO ORBIT

The surface of Earth is curved. In fact, Earth is just a really BIG ball of rock. When a rocket lifts off it will usually go into orbit around Earth, where it circles in a regular and repeating path.

Earth's curve allows rockets to orbit. An object in orbit follows a curved path as gravity pulls it towards the surface of Earth, but at the same time Earth is also curving away from it. Let's explore how orbits work.

YOU WILL NEED:

- a tennis ball
- an old pair of tights
- scissors

1 Hold the tennis ball at arm's length. Let it go and watch it drop to the floor. The force of gravity from Earth pulls on the ball so that it falls straight down.

2 Now ask a friend to throw the same ball gently away from themselves horizontally. From the side, watch the path of the ball carefully and note where it lands. What do you notice? You should see that the ball follows a curved path. The ball is moving forwards, but the force of gravity still pulls it down.

3 Ask your friend to throw the ball harder. Notice that it lands further away but, more importantly, it follows a shallower curve before landing.

If you stood on top of the tallest mountain and threw the ball at 8 km/s, then the ball would follow a curved path as gravity pulls it down. That curved path would match the curve of Earth's surface. In other words, the ball would constantly fall towards Earth, but Earth would constantly fall away from the ball, too. The ball would be in orbit!

4 Cut one leg off the pair of tights and push the ball down into the toe.

5 In an open space, swing the ball in a big circle. The ball moves away from you in a straight line unless something makes it go somewhere else. (This is Isaac Newton's first law of motion.)

The force of gravity (your hand pulling on the tights) causes the ball's path to turn in a circle, orbiting your hand.

SPACE FACT

It is not only rockets travelling around Earth that are in orbit. Earth is orbited by our Moon, Earth is in orbit around the Sun and the Sun is in orbit around the centre of our galaxy – the Milky Way.

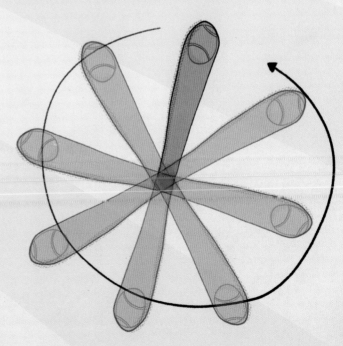

MAKE WATER WEIGHTLESS

If you watch a video of an astronaut in space, you will see them floating gently around. You might think that they have escaped the pull of Earth's gravity, but astronauts float because they are in a state known as free-fall.

Objects in orbit are constantly in free-fall because they are being pulled down by the gravity of whatever they are orbiting. At the same time, the object being orbited is curving away from them at the same speed (see pages 22–23). They seem weightless, because everything else around them is falling at the exact same speed. You can explore weightlessness with a cup of water, but do it outside because you might get wet!

YOU WILL NEED:

- a paper or plastic cup
- scissors
- a jug of water

1 Ask an adult to help you cut a small hole in the side of the cup. The hole should be close to the bottom of the cup.

2 Take the jug of water outside, place a finger over the hole and fill the cup two thirds full. Take your finger away and watch what happens. A steady stream of water will pour out of the hole because gravity is pulling it down. The cup is not pulled down by gravity because your hand is holding it up.

3 Now place your finger over the hole and again fill the cup two thirds full of water.

4 This time, gently let go of the cup as you pull your finger away from the hole. Watch carefully. Look out for the splash as the cup hits the ground!

5 You should notice that as the cup falls with the water, none of the water pours out of the hole. Like the astronaut in space, the water is free-falling inside the cup, making it seem weightless.

SPACE FACT

Water in space is a very tricky thing to deal with. It is free-falling, so it is impossible to make it stay inside a cup. Instead it floats around and forms balls of water. Astronauts can have lots of fun floating around in the ISS trying to catch floating balls of water!

BECOME A ROCKET BOOSTER

Have you noticed that all space rockets have a funnel at the bottom? If you squeeze the gas from a rocket engine through the narrow part of this funnel, the gas goes through that gap faster. The speed that a rocket can zoom through space is determined by the speed the gas shoots out the bottom. Using a funnel to make the gas escape more quickly makes the rocket go even faster!

This is known as the Venturi effect and is named after the Italian scientist who discovered it – Giovanni Battista Venturi (1746–1822). You can explore the Venturi effect for yourself in this experiment.

YOU WILL NEED:

- a glass (or other container)
- some water
- a straw
- scissors
- sticky tape

1 Fill the glass with water up to about 2 cm from the top.

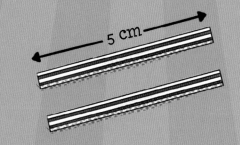

5 cm

2 Cut the straw into two pieces. Both pieces should be about 5 cm in length.

3 Tape one piece of straw inside the glass. One end in the water and the other end sticking up above the rim of the glass. The straw is your funnel.

4 Take everything outside. Place the glass on a table or other surface so that you can get down low next to it. Hold the other straw horizontally, so that it is just over the open end of the funnel. You may need to experiment a bit to get this right.

5 Blow through the horizontal straw to see the Venturi effect in action! When the water (or gas out of a rocket) escapes out of the funnel, it causes the pressure in the funnel to go down.
This in turn causes the water to be sucked up and sprayed out in front of you!

CREATE
You can use the Venturi effect to blow water-based paint onto a piece of paper to make cool art.

SPACE FACT
The *Saturn V* rockets that took the Apollo astronauts to the Moon would never have got them there without the funnels boosting the speed, or thrust, of the rocket engines.

LAUNCH THE ULTIMATE ROCKET!

In the previous experiments, you have found out how to design rockets, how to use chemical reactions to push rockets into space and even how to make rockets go faster. It is now time to build the ULTIMATE rocket! This activity is best performed outside and well away from any buildings or power lines, as your rocket might reach the height of a house!

YOU WILL NEED:

- a clean, empty 2-litre drinks bottle
- a cork
- four straws (not bendy ones)
- sticky tape
- some white vinegar
- four teaspoons of baking soda
- kitchen roll

1

Make sure the cork fits the opening of the bottle. Remove the cork.

2

Tape the four straws around the neck end of the bottle. They should all stick up about 3 cm higher than the neck. The bottle should stand up on the straws without wobbling or falling over. Next, fill the bottle about a third full of white vinegar.

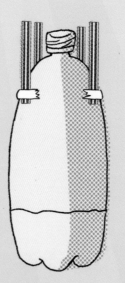

3

Put four heaped teaspoons of baking soda onto a piece of kitchen roll. Then roll it up, so it will fit into the neck of the bottle without the baking soda falling out. (Don't put it in the bottle yet!)

RED ALERT!

Ask an adult to help you with this experiment. It must be performed in an outside open space!

4 Now for the fun bit! These next two steps need to be done quickly and you will need an adult to help you. Put the rolled up kitchen paper into the bottle so that it drops into the vinegar and quickly put in the cork. DO NOT lean over the rocket as you do this.

5 Quickly turn the rocket over, place it on the floor and stand well back!

GO FURTHER

Try and make your rocket go higher by fixing a cardboard nose cone to it. This will cut down the air resistance and make it go higher. You might also want to try adding some fins to the rocket too, so that it flies straighter.

SPACE FACT

When it has run out of fuel, our Ultimate Rocket falls back down to the ground and can be used again. Many rockets have parts that cannot be used again, while others have parts that fall back to Earth on parachutes and are re-used.

29

GLOSSARY

AERODYNAMIC a shape that helps to reduce the force of drag on an object

ANTACID a medicine that helps to reduce acid levels in the stomach

DRAG a force that slows down moving objects

ENGINE a machine that converts power into motion

EXOTHERMIC a chemical reaction that gives off energy, usually as heat

FORCE the pushes and pulls that cause things to move

FUNNEL a pipe with a wide end and a narrow end

GAS one of the three main states of matter. A gas can expand, squeeze, and flow from one place to another.

GRAVITY a force that tries to pull two objects together

HYDROGEN a flammable gas with no smell or colour. It is a chemical element usually represented by the letter H.

MATTER stuff that makes up everything around us and is usually either a solid, a liquid or a gas

MOLECULES the building blocks of all matter. Each molecule is made of a group of atoms.

NEWTONS the unit of measurement used for force

ORBIT a circular or oval path one object follows around another

OXYGEN a gas with no smell or colour that is essential for life on Earth. It is a chemical element usually represented by the letter O.

PARACHUTE a sheet of material that fills with air as it falls, causing it to fall more slowly

PARTICLE a tiny object that makes up matter. Atoms are the smallest particles

PRESSURE the effect of a force being applied against something

RESISTANCE an effect where something is slowed down or stopped by something else

SOLAR SYSTEM the planets, moons and other space objects that orbit the Sun

SPEED OF LIGHT maximum possible speed of any matter, which is 299,792, 458 m/s

STABLE something that is not likely to wobble or fall over

UNBALANCED not of equal amounts

YEAST a microscopic fungus made of cells that can reproduce, and change sugar into alcohol and carbon dioxide

FURTHER INFORMATION

BOOKS

Ground Control to Major Tim: The space adventures of Major Tim Peake by Clive Gifford (Wayland, 2017)

How To Build: Rockets by Louise Derrington (Franklin Watts, 2016)

It'll Never Work: Rockets and Space Travel: An accidental history of inventions by Jon Richards (Franklin Watts, 2016)

Planet Earth: Journey into Space by Michael Bright (Wayland, 2016)

PLACES TO VISIT

National Space Centre, Leicester
Science Museum, London
Glasgow Science Centre, Glasgow
Winchester Science Centre, Winchester

WEBSITES

The NASA Kids website has loads of interactive space activities, such as building your own rocket and trying your hand at driving a Martian buggy.
www.nasa.gov/kidsclub/index.html

BBC Bitesize is a great website with lots of curriculum based science activities.
www.bbc.co.uk/bitesize

The ESA Kids website has plenty of fun and games for kids to explore space.
www.esa.int/kids/en/home

Note to parents and teachers: Every effort has been made by the Publishers to ensure that the websites in this book are suitable for children, that they are of the highest educational value, and that they contain no inappropriate or offensive material. However, because of the nature of the Internet, it is impossible to guarantee that the contents of these sites will not be altered. We strongly advise that Internet access is supervised by a responsible adult.

INDEX